NEVER HAVE I EVER...

An Exciting and Sexy Game for Adults

HOT AND DIRTY EDITION

J.R. James

All rights reserved. No portion of this book may be reproduced in any form without permission from the publisher, except as permitted by U.S. copyright law.

This book is for entertainment purposes only. This book is not intended, nor should the reader consider it, to be relational advice for any situation. The author makes no representations or warranties with respect to accuracy, fitness, completeness, or applicability of the contents of this book.

Copyright © 2019 Love & Desire Press

All rights reserved.

ISBN 13: 978-1-952328-07-7

Spice up your love life even more, and explore all the discussion books for couples by J.R. James:

Love and Relationship Books for Couples

Would You Rather...? The Romantic Conversation Game for Couples (Love and Romance Edition)

Sexy Game Books for Couples

Would You Rather...? The Naughty Conversation Game for Couples (Hot and Sexy Edition)

Truth or Dare? The Sexy Game of Naughty Choices (Hot and Wild Edition)

Never Have I Ever... An Exciting and Sexy Game for Adults (Hot and Dirty Edition)

The Hot or Not Quiz for Couples: The Sexy Game of Naughty Questions and Revealing Answers

Pillow Talk: The Sexy Game of Naughty Trivia Questions for Couples

The Naughty Newlywed Game: A Sexy Game of Questions for Couples

Sexy Discussion Books for Couples

Let's Talk Sexy: Essential Conversation Starters to Explore Your Lover's Secret Desires and Transform Your Sex Life

All **THREE** *Let's Talk About...* sexy question books in one massive volume for one low price. Save now!

Let's Talk About... Sexual Fantasies and Desires: Questions and Conversation Starters for Couples Exploring Their Sexual Interests

Let's Talk About... Non-Monogamy: Questions and Conversation Starters for Couples Exploring Open Relationships, Swinging, or Polyamory

Let's Talk About... Kinks and Fetishes: Questions and Conversation Starters for Couples Exploring Their Sexual Wild Side

Change your sex life forever through the power of sexy fun with your spouse, partner, or lover!

www.sexygamesforcouples.com

Sexy Vacations for Couples
https://geni.us/Passion

HOW TO PLAY THE GAME

The rules for this game are very simple, if a little different than the typical *Never Have I Ever..* game:

There needs to be at least two people to play. (It's a great game for new couples to learn about each other!) If you and your partner are really adventurous, try playing with another couple, or even more people at a party. The more people, the more fun!

Each page has a statement that begins with "Never have I ever…". One player should read the statement in its entirety. Each player will then consider if the statement is true for them, and if it is, they will hold up a finger. For example: Seth and Lucy are playing together. Seth reads, "Never have I ever… Had a threesome." Seth has never had a ménage a trois, so he doesn't do anything. Lucy has had a threesome, so she holds up one finger. (You can use anything to keep score, not just fingers.) After ten statements, there is a prize page. **Whoever has the highest score with the most fingers up is the winner of the round and wins the prize.** It's a game that rewards a player's naughty, sexy past! The player with the lowest score needs to follow the directions on the prize page to reward the winner. If there are more than two people playing, then the winner is the person with the highest score, and the loser is the one with the lowest score. After the prize is completed, reset the scores and start a new round.

As you spend time discussing the answers, you'll soon you'll find yourselves smiling, laughing, and enjoying the sexually charged conversation. Who knows? You may even discover new sexual possibilities for your relationship. Just have fun, because it's the game where everyone wins!

ROUND 1

<u>1</u>

Never have I ever...

Had sex while at school or work.

<u>2</u>

Never have I ever...

Accidentally sent nudes or naughty texts to the wrong person.

3
Never have I ever…
Masturbated in front of someone else.

4
Never have I ever…
Watched another couple having sex.

5
Never have I ever...
Had a fantasy involving one of my teachers.

6
Never have I ever...
Made a sex video.

7

Never have I ever…
Used food during sex.

8

Never have I ever…
Had sex in a public area.

_9_

Never have I ever…

Slept with someone without knowing their first name.

_10_

Never have I ever…

Given or received a golden shower.

Prize Page

The winner of this round gets to choose what the loser has to wear, or not wear, for the next three rounds.

ROUND 2

_11_

Never have I ever…

Had sex with a screamer or a biter.

_12_

Never have I ever…

Faked an orgasm.

_13_

Never have I ever…

Lied to someone about how good they were in bed.

_14_

Never have I ever…

Left work early to have sex.

_15_

Never have I ever…

Given a sexy striptease set to music.

_16_

Never have I ever…

Mistakenly called someone the wrong name in bed.

17

Never have I ever…

Sucked someone's toes or had my toes sucked.

18

Never have I ever…

Flirted with someone when I knew they were taken.

19

Never have I ever…

Watched somebody else masturbate.

20

Never have I ever…

Had sex with someone with terrible body odor.

Prize Page

The loser has to try and make the winner moan in pleasure within two minutes. You can do it in whatever way you think will work the quickest.

ROUND 3

21
Never have I ever…
Gone more than a year between sexual encounters.

22
Never have I ever…
Had anal sex.

23

Never have I ever…

Fooled around with someone famous.

24

Never have I ever…

Given or received a handjob in a public place.

_25_

Never have I ever…

Given or received a lap dance.

_26_

Never have I ever…

Had a one night stand.

_27_

Never have I ever...

Had a threesome.

_28_

Never have I ever...

Watched a porn video together with a lover.

29

Never have I ever…

Had a sexual experience with someone of the same sex. (Alternate: With someone of the opposite sex.)

30

Never have I ever…

Swapped partners with another couple.

Prize Page

The loser of this round has to send a very sexy selfie with a dirty text to the winner's phone.

ROUND 4

_31_

Never have I ever…

Had sex while I was tied up.

_32_

Never have I ever…

Joined the mile high club. (Had a sexual experience on a plane.)

33

Never have I ever…

Been to a nude beach or resort.

34

Never have I ever…

Had a sexual fling with someone ten years older or younger than myself.

35

Never have I ever…

Been handcuffed to a bed.

36

Never have I ever…

Had a sexual fantasy about a co-worker.

37
Never have I ever…
Had sex in a pool or hot tub.

38
Never have I ever…
Had an "innocent" massage lead to sex.

39

Never have I ever…

Had pity sex with someone.

40

Never have I ever…

Had a crush on a friend's parent.

Prize Page

The loser of this round needs to softly tease the winner's chest, neck, and ears with their lips and tongue for one minute.

ROUND 5

41

Never have I ever…

Had sex while I was really drunk.

42

Never have I ever…

Had sex in a quiet public location, such as a library or a museum.

_43_

Never have I ever…

Played the role as a lover's sex slave.

_44_

Never have I ever…

Licked someone's anus, or had mine licked.

_45_
Never have I ever…
Read an erotic novel.

_46_
Never have I ever…
Kicked someone out right after sex.

47

Never have I ever…

Fallen asleep during sex.

48

Never have I ever…

Slept with a stripper.

_**49**_
Never have I ever…
Had sex in the woods.

_**50**_
Never have I ever…
Eavesdropped on someone else having sex.

Prize Page

The winner of this round gets to pick any part of their body and have the loser sensually and seductively kiss it for two minutes.

ROUND 6

_51_

Never have I ever…

Been spanked with a belt, whip, or paddle.

_52_

Never have I ever…

Had a sexual encounter in a public restroom.

53
Never have I ever…
Done a body shot.

54
Never have I ever…
Had a sexual fantasy come true.

55

Never have I ever…

Bought a sex toy.

56

Never have I ever…

Had a sexual experience in a darkened movie theater.

57
Never have I ever…
Licked chocolate syrup or whipped cream off of someone.

58
Never have I ever…
Watched a significant other have sex with someone else.

59

Never have I ever...

Tried a sexual position
from the Kama Sutra.

60

Never have I ever...

Played strip poker.

Prize Page

The winner of this round gets to choose a food item, place it anywhere on their body, and have the loser lick it off of them. (The winner can switch roles if they so choose, and lick it off of the loser instead.)

ROUND 7

_61_

Never have I ever…
Been to a sex club.

_62_

Never have I ever…
Had sex while blindfolded.

63

Never have I ever…

Flirted with someone else in front of a significant other.

64

Never have I ever…

Had sex without any kissing involved.

65
Never have I ever…
Tried Tantric sex.

66
Never have I ever…
Been to any sort of sex class.

67

Never have I ever…

Had someone take sexy photos of me.

68

Never have I ever…

Had sex more than four times in a day.

_69_

Never have I ever…

Shaved someone else's pubic area.

_70_

Never have I ever…

Given a partner a "hall pass" (temporary permission to sleep with someone else).

Prize Page

The loser has to give the winner a foot massage for two minutes while telling the them all the ways they are amazing in bed. (If you don't know how they are in bed, then make it up.)

ROUND 8

71
Never have I ever…
Had sex on a beach.

72
Never have I ever…
Used a sex swing.

__73__
Never have I ever…
Teased a lover with ice cubes.

__74__
Never have I ever…
Tried any kind of BDSM during sex.

75

Never have I ever…

Visited a strip club.

76

Never have I ever…

Had sex in front of an open window.

77
Never have I ever…
Had sex with more than five people in a year.

78
Never have I ever…
Been walked in on while having sex.

79

Never have I ever…

Used an internet video camera to have "sex."

80

Never have I ever…

Made someone orgasm in under a minute.

Prize Page

The loser has to gently tease and pleasure the winner using only their hands and fingertips for three minutes.

ROUND 9

81
Never have I ever…
Made out with two people at the same time.

82
Never have I ever…
Been gagged during sex.

83

Never have I ever...

Had sex with a virgin.

84

Never have I ever...

Had a sexual fantasy about an animated character.

85
Never have I ever…
Had my nipples or genitals pierced.

86
Never have I ever…
Been injured during sex.

87
Never have I ever…
Gone more than a month without masturbating.

88
Never have I ever…
Slept in the nude all night.

_89_

Never have I ever…

Talked dirty to a lover during sex.

_90_

Never have I ever…

Roleplay while in costume.

Prize Page

The loser has to orally pleasure the winner for two minutes in whatever way they wish.

ROUND 10

_91_

Never have I ever…

Worn a chastity device.

_92_

Never have I ever…

Participated in an orgy.

_93_

Never have I ever…
Had sex on a boat.

_94_

Never have I ever…
Made out with a complete stranger.

95

Never have I ever…

Been caught masturbating.

96

Never have I ever…

Flirted with a teacher or a boss.

__97__
Never have I ever…
Made a purchase at an Adult store.

__98__
Never have I ever…
Made someone orgasm while they were fully clothed.

99

Never have I ever…

Worn a very sexy
Halloween costume.

100

Never have I ever…

Flashed someone.

Prize Page

The winner of this round gets a sensual massage from the loser for five minutes.

ROUND
11

__*101*__

Never have I ever…

Paid or got paid for sex.

__*102*__

Never have I ever…

Been skinny dipping.

103

Never have I ever…

Had phone sex with a lover.

104

Never have I ever…

Had sex in a moving car.

_105_
Never have I ever…
Given someone a hickey on purpose.

_106_
Never have I ever…
Masturbated while at work or school.

107

Never have I ever…

Gone streaking.

108

Never have I ever…

Stopped eating a meal in order to have sex.

109
Never have I ever…
Sunbathed in the nude.

110
Never have I ever…
Tried to get someone to orgasm as quickly as possible in order to be done with sex.

Prize Page

The winner of this round gets to choose what they'd like the loser to do for the next one minute.

ROUND 12

111

Never have I ever…

Played dirty Truth or Dare.

112

Never have I ever…

Taken a shower or a bath with someone.

113
Never have I ever…
Slept with someone twice my age.

114
Never have I ever…
Bought sexy lingerie or underwear for someone.

115

Never have I ever...

Used flavored lube or condoms.

116

Never have I ever...

Peeked at someone while they were changing.

117
Never have I ever...
Used Tinder or other app to get laid.

118
Never have I ever...
Slept with someone I wasn't attracted to.

_119_

Never have I ever…

Had someone accidentally find dirty pictures on my phone.

_120_

Never have I ever…

Had revenge or rebound sex.

Prize Page

The winner of this round gets a sexy striptease and lap dance from the loser. The winner gets to pick out the song they have to dance to.

ROUND 13

121
Never have I ever…
Skipped wearing underwear for the day.

122
Never have I ever…
Cheated on a boyfriend or girlfriend.

123
Never have I ever…
Lied about something in order to get laid.

124
Never have I ever…
Screwed around in an elevator.

125
Never have I ever…
Slept with someone within an hour of meeting them.

126
Never have I ever…
Been choked during sex.

127
Never have I ever…
Completed an entire sexual encounter without ever lying down.

128
Never have I ever…
Slept in a bed with four or more people.

129
Never have I ever…
Had sex in the back of a pickup truck.

130
Never have I ever…
Done it in a sleeping bag.

Reverse Prize Page

Including this round, identify which player has lost the most rounds during the entire game.

This deprived individual needs some extra sexy experiences. For this last round, the most winning player of the game has to make one sexual fantasy come true for the player who lost the most rounds.

Spice up your love life even more, and explore all the discussion books for couples by J.R. James:

Love and Relationship Books for Couples

Would You Rather...? The Romantic Conversation Game for Couples (Love and Romance Edition)

Sexy Game Books for Couples

Would You Rather...? The Naughty Conversation Game for Couples (Hot and Sexy Edition)

Truth or Dare? The Sexy Game of Naughty Choices (Hot and Wild Edition)

Never Have I Ever... An Exciting and Sexy Game for Adults (Hot and Dirty Edition)

The Hot or Not Quiz for Couples: The Sexy Game of Naughty Questions and Revealing Answers

Pillow Talk: The Sexy Game of Naughty Trivia Questions for Couples

The Naughty Newlywed Game: A Sexy Game of Questions for Couples

Sexy Discussion Books for Couples

Let's Talk Sexy: Essential Conversation Starters to Explore Your Lover's Secret Desires and Transform Your Sex Life

All **THREE** *Let's Talk About...* sexy question books in one massive volume for one low price. Save now!

Let's Talk About... Sexual Fantasies and Desires: Questions and Conversation Starters for Couples Exploring Their Sexual Interests

Let's Talk About... Non-Monogamy: Questions and Conversation Starters for Couples Exploring Open Relationships, Swinging, or Polyamory

Let's Talk About... Kinks and Fetishes: Questions and Conversation Starters for Couples Exploring Their Sexual Wild Side

Change your sex life forever through the power of sexy fun with your spouse, partner, or lover!

www.sexygamesforcouples.com

Sexy Vacations for Couples
https://geni.us/Passion

ABOUT THE AUTHOR

J.R. James is a West Coast Health Professional who has a passion for bringing couples closer together and recharging their sexual intimacy. Erotic discussion is a powerfully sexy thing, and his conversation starter books have helped many couples reach new and sexually exciting heights in their relationships!

Sexy conversation with your partner is a magical, bonding experience. Through these best-selling question books, couples can find an easy way to engage in open and honest sexual discussion with each other. The result is a relationship that is both erotically charged and sexually liberating.

www.ingramcontent.com/pod-product-compliance
Lightning Source LLC
Chambersburg PA
CBHW071723020426
42333CB00017B/2373